T0413999

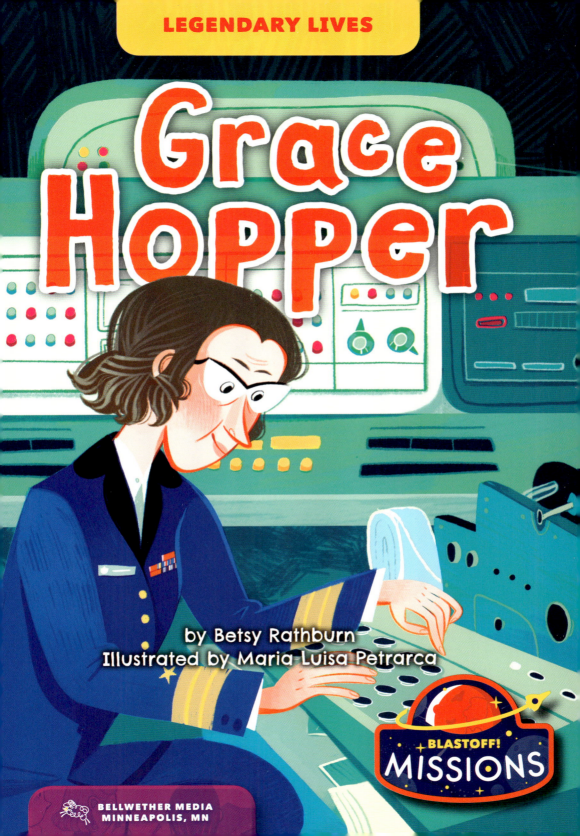

Grace Hopper

by Betsy Rathburn
Illustrated by Maria Luisa Petrarca

BLASTOFF!
MISSIONS

BELLWETHER MEDIA
MINNEAPOLIS, MN

Blastoff! Missions takes you on a learning adventure! Colorful illustrations and exciting narratives highlight cool facts about our world and beyond. Read the mission goals and follow the narrative to gain knowledge, build reading skills, and have fun!

Traditional Nonfiction

Narrative Nonfiction

Blastoff! Universe

MISSION GOALS

> FIND YOUR SIGHT WORDS IN THE BOOK.

> LEARN ABOUT GRACE HOPPER'S LIFE.

> LEARN HOW GRACE HOPPER'S WORK HELPED DURING WORLD WAR II.

This edition first published in 2025 by Bellwether Media, Inc.

No part of this publication may be reproduced in whole or in part without written permission of the publisher. For information regarding permission, write to Bellwether Media, Inc., Attention: Permissions Department, 6012 Blue Circle Drive, Minnetonka, MN 55343.

Library of Congress Cataloging-in-Publication Data

LC record for Grace Hopper available at: https://lccn.loc.gov/2024041929

Editor: Rebecca Sabelko   Designer: Andrea Schneider

Printed in the United States of America, North Mankato, MN.

This is **Blastoff Jimmy**! He is here to help you on your mission and share fun facts along the way!

Table of Contents

Meet Grace Hopper

Grace Hopper is working hard. She is **programming** a computer! Her work helps people do their jobs!

computer

▶ JIMMY SAYS ◀

Grace was awarded the Presidential Medal of Freedom in 2016.

An Early Start

It is the 1910s. Young Grace lives in New York. She loves seeing how things work. She takes apart a clock. But now it does not work.

Her parents **encourage** her to keep trying!

Now Grace goes to Vassar College.
She studies many subjects.

She helps other students with math
and **physics**.

Grace now teaches math at Vassar College. She expects her students to study hard.

Grace also works toward a **doctorate** in math. She earns it in 1934.

The United States has entered **World War II**. Grace wants to help. She joins the U.S. Naval **Reserve**!

The Navy has Grace work on a computer. It is called the Mark I. She must become a computer programmer.

Grace learns quickly. Her math skills help. Her work gives the military important information!

It is now 1945. The war is over. Grace keeps working on the Mark I.

She helps write rules for using the computer. It is the first computer **manual** ever made!

Grace works on other projects. She helps make UNIVAC I. It is the first computer used outside the military in the U.S.

She works to create **COBOL** in 1959. This **programming language** is still used today!

COBOL programming language
0718
0719
0720
0721
0722
0723
0724
0740
0803
F00087
BF1940
000000
B01940
Q00123
LF1833
000728
000740
C00803
000738
AH1829
+
12C
INSTRU
FROM
VERB

Grace becomes a **rear admiral** in 1985. Her military service ends the next year. She is 79.

Grace was a computer **pioneer**. She won many honors. Her work changed the world!

Grace Hopper Profile

Born

December 9, 1906, in New York, New York

Died

January 1, 1992

Accomplishments

Mathematician and computer programmer who served in the U.S. Naval Reserve from 1943 to 1986

Timeline

1928: Earns a degree in math and physics from Vassar College

1934: Earns a doctorate in math from Yale University

1944: Begins working on the Mark I as a member of the U.S. Naval Reserve

1959: Works to create the COBOL programming language

1985: Becomes a rear admiral, with her military service ending the next year

Glossary

COBOL—an English-like programming language invented in 1959 that could work on many different machines; COBOL is short for common, business-oriented language.

doctorate—the highest degree at a college; a doctorate is also called a PhD.

encourage—to give the help needed to accomplish a goal

manual—a book of rules that explains how to use a machine

physics—a science that deals with matter, energy, heat, light, electricity, motion, and sound

pioneer—a person who is among the first to do something

programming—writing computer programs using a programming language

programming language—a set of rules used to make computer programs

rear admiral—a senior officer in the U.S. Navy

reserve—a military force that is only called to action in an emergency

World War II—the war fought from 1939 to 1945 that involved many countries

To Learn More

AT THE LIBRARY

Burns, Kylie. *Coding with Robotics.* Minneapolis, Minn.: Bellwether Media, 2024.

Noll, Elizabeth. *Computer Programmer.* Minneapolis, Minn.: Bellwether Media, 2023.

Proudfit, Benjamin. *Grace Hopper and the Computer.* New York, N.Y.: Gareth Stevens Publishing, 2023.

ON THE WEB

FACTSURFER

Factsurfer.com gives you a safe, fun way to find more information.

1. Go to www.factsurfer.com.

2. Enter "Grace Hopper" into the search box and click 🔍.

3. Select your book cover to see a list of related content.

BEYOND THE MISSION

> WHAT FACT FROM THE BOOK DID YOU THINK WAS THE MOST INTERESTING?

> WHAT QUESTIONS WOULD YOU HAVE LIKED TO ASK GRACE ABOUT HER LIFE?

> WHAT WOULD YOU LIKE TO LEARN ABOUT COMPUTERS?

Index